At the Optician

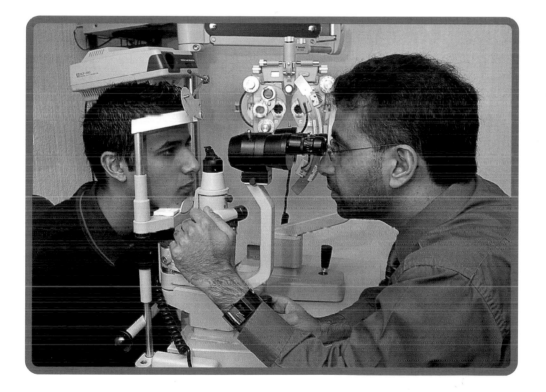

Deborah Chancellor

Photographs: Chris Fairclough

FRANKLIN WATTS
LONDON·SYDNEY

This edition 2007

First published in 2003 by
Franklin Watts
338 Euston Road
London NW1 3BH

Franklin Watts Australia
Level 17/207 Kent Street
Sydney NSW 2000

© Franklin Watts 2003
Dewey Decimal Classification Number 617.7

A CIP catalogue record for this book is available
from the British Library.

ISBN 978 0 7496 7271 3

Series Editor: Jackie Hamley
Cover Design: Peter Scoulding
Design: Ian Thompson
Illustrator: David Burroughs

Photos
All commissioned photographs by Chris Fairclough.
The publishers would like to thank the following
for permission to use photographs:
BSIP, LAURENT / Science Photo Library 21 (top)

Every attempt has been made to clear copyright. Should there be any inadvertent
omission, please apply to the publisher for rectification.

The author and publisher would especially like to thank the team and
customers at Evington Eyecare for giving their help and time so generously.

Printed in Malaysia

Franklin Watts is a division of Hachette Children's Books.

Contents

Meet the team

■ **If we need to have our eyes tested, we go to an optician's practice. The person who tests our eyes is called an optometrist.**

Riyaz is an **optometrist**. He works at an **optician's practice** called Evington Eyecare in Leicester, England. The practice opened eleven years ago. It now has about eight thousand patients.

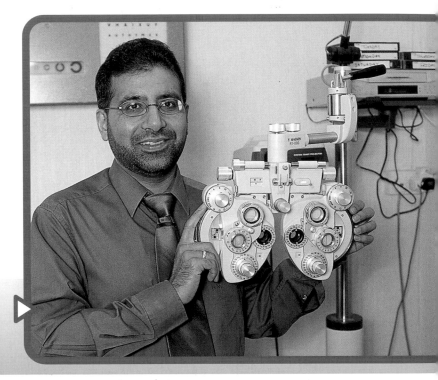

Riyaz is trained to test people's eyesight.

Toni tells a patient that their new glasses are ready to be collected.

Other people work at the optician's practice, too. Toni is a **dispenser**. She makes sure that people have the right **lenses** fitted in their glasses. She also orders **contact lenses** for patients.

Hayley is one of the receptionists. She makes appointments for patients and looks after their eye test records.

Hayley checks some **patient records** on the computer.

This is the team who work together to look after people's eyes.

1 Riyaz, optometrist
2 Toni, assistant manager and dispenser
3 Hayley, receptionist
4 Joe, part-time receptionist

■ Every day, many people come into the optician's practice. They may want an eye test, or new frames for glasses.

Deborah wants to make an appointment for an eye test.

When people arrive, they usually go to the reception desk. They can speak to the receptionist to arrange an appointment, or to pick up glasses or contact lenses they have ordered.

Frames for glasses are on display next to the reception desk. There are lots of different styles to choose from.

This large, light area allows people to look at all the frames.

Eye tests take place in a separate room, away from the reception desk.

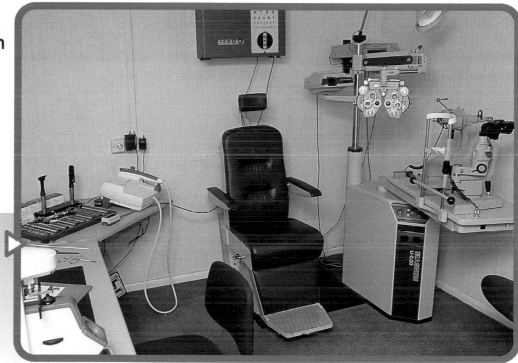

Riyaz keeps his special **optical equipment** in the testing room.

The eye is made up of different parts which work together to allow us to see. Some people's eyes do not work properly and they need to wear glasses or contact lenses to see well. The lenses in glasses or contact lenses work with the **lens** in the eye to correct the person's eyesight.

This drawing shows the different parts of the eye. Light enters the eye through the **pupil**. The light then passes through the lens, which **focuses** it onto the **retina** to form an image. The optic nerve sends messages from the retina to the brain, and the brain works out what the eye is looking at.

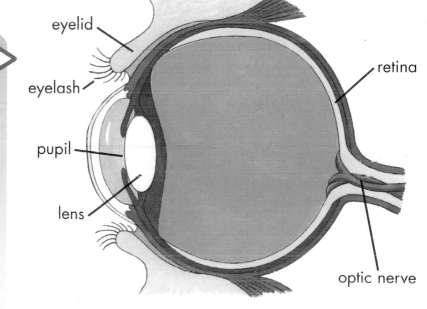

eyelid

eyelash

pupil

lens

retina

optic nerve

Making an appointment

If you need to have an eye test, you can come into the optician's practice or phone up to make an appointment.

Hayley arranges appointments. She writes the date and time of the appointment in the reception desk diary.

Hayley is arranging an appointment over the phone.

Deborah's appointment is in a few days' time.

When the appointment has been made, Hayley gives or sends the patient a card, which shows when the appointment is.

> *Saturday is our busiest day of the week. People have more time to come in at the weekend.*
> **Hayley, receptionist**

Riyaz likes his patients to come in for an eye test at least once a year. When a patient is due for an eye test, Hayley sends them a reminder card. This card invites them to make another appointment.

FACT

Short- and long-sighted

▷ Lots of people are short- or long-sighted.

▷ People who are **short-sighted** can't focus on things in the distance and often need glasses for driving.

▷ People who are **long-sighted** can't focus on things that are close to them and often need glasses for reading.

Riyaz sees about sixteen patients every day.

Riyaz's appointment diary is always very full. At the beginning of each day, Riyaz checks the diary to see who is coming in for an eye test.

New patients

New patients have to fill in a registration form. They give important details about their eyesight and general health on this form.

Deborah has not had an eye test at Evington Eyecare before. When she arrives for her first appointment, Joe writes her name and address on the registration form.

Joe fills in the registration form so that Deborah can take it with her when she has her eye test.

At Deborah's first eye test, Riyaz asks about her eyesight and health. He needs to know if any of her relatives have difficulty seeing, because sight problems can run in families.

The information on the registration form is written up on Deborah's patient record card.

After Riyaz has tested the patient's eyesight, Hayley files the patient record card.

The patient record cards are kept in filing cabinets behind the reception desk. They are also stored on the computer. Patient records are kept for many years.

Some people, such as children and certain students can have free eye tests. Jackie is a student in Leicester. She needs an eye test, and shows her student identity card to prove that she does not have to pay.

Jackie often uses a computer for her studies. Using a computer a lot can strain your eyesight, so she is making an appointment for an eye test.

🎲 **Riyaz tests eyesight in different ways. If patients already wear glasses, Riyaz finds out if their eyesight has changed.**

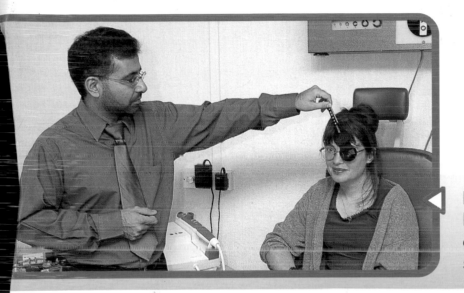

Riyaz begins Deborah's eye test by checking how well she can see with her glasses.

Riyaz tests each eye separately. He covers up Deborah's left eye to check how well she can see with her right eye.

Then Deborah takes off her glasses. She looks through a series of different lenses. These lenses are like the ones put into glasses.

Riyaz tries lenses of different strengths, to work out which ones will help Deborah see as well as possible.

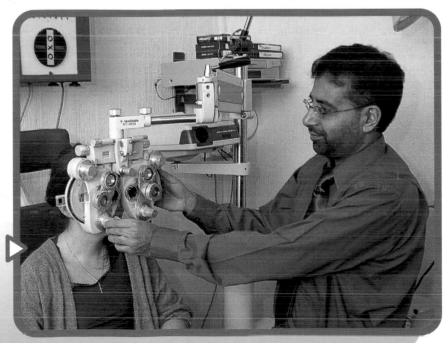

Deborah looks through the lenses for a number of tests. One test is a letter chart, showing lines of letters which get smaller in size.

Deborah's eyesight has got weaker, so she needs stronger lenses in her glasses. Riyaz writes down her new **prescription** on her record card. This describes the strength and type of lenses Deborah needs.

The top picture shows how Deborah sees the letter chart without her glasses. The lower picture shows how she sees it with them. ▷

During an eye test, Riyaz checks that his patient's eyes are healthy. Eye disease can lead to serious eyesight problems. Riyaz uses special equipment to look right inside the eyes.

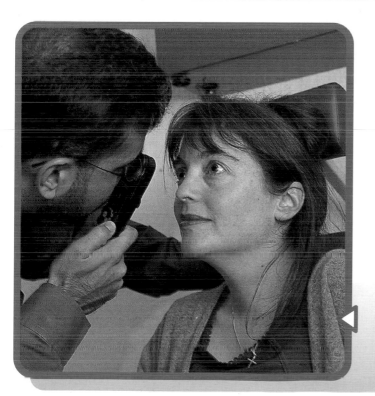

◁ Riyaz looks through an instrument called an opthalmoscope to check the back of Deborah's eyes.

Children's eyesight

■ **Some eyesight problems can begin at a very young age, so children should have their first eye test before they start school.**

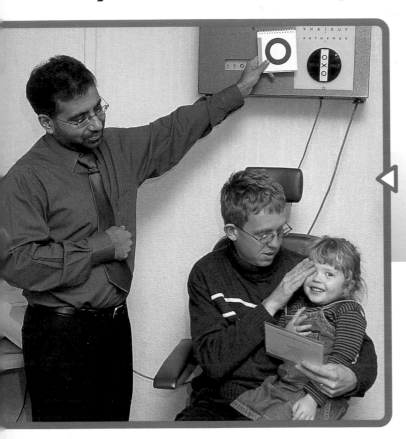

Most small children can't read letters, so Riyaz uses matching cards with pictures and shapes on them to test their eyesight.

The card Riyaz is holding is reflected in a mirror in front of Imogen. She is asked if it has the same shape on it as the card her dad is holding.

Riyaz asks Femi to look at the stick. As Riyaz moves the stick, he covers each of Femi's eyes in turn. This helps show if Femi has a squint.

Riyaz always checks whether a child has a **squint**. This means he tests that both eyes can look in the same direction at something. A child with a squint will need to wear special glasses to correct the condition.

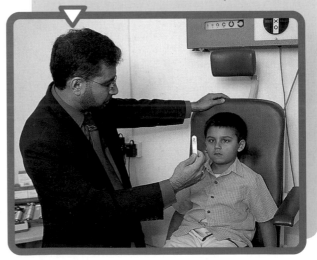

Some children have a **lazy eye**. This means that one eye has weaker muscles and can't focus as well as the other.

Femi has a lazy eye. His strong eye is covered so that his lazy eye has to work harder. This will strengthen the muscles in the lazy eye.

Femi was given a sticker for being a good patient.

People who are **colour-blind** can't tell the difference between certain colours. Riyaz always tests children between eight and twelve years old for colour-blindness.

FACT

▷ One in twelve boys is colour-blind.

▷ One in two hundred girls is colour-blind.

▷ People who are colour-blind can find it hard to tell the difference between:

▷ red and green

▷ blue and yellow

Riyaz uses patterns of coloured dots to test for colour-blindness. He asks the patient to read out the numbers shown in the patterns.

Young people's eyesight can change quickly. This is why all children should have check-ups every six to twelve months.

Femi wears glasses. When he comes for his regular check-up, Riyaz finds out whether his lens prescription has changed since his last visit. Riyaz asks Femi to look through trial lenses at some letters and pictures.

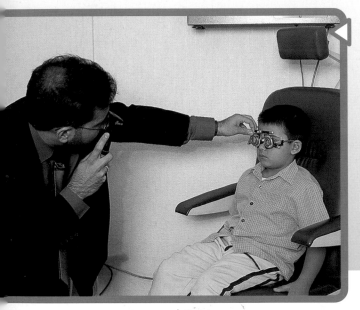

Riyaz uses a special instrument called a retinoscope to look in Femi's eyes and see where light is being focused.

Riyaz keeps his trial lenses in a special box.

The trial lenses are all slightly different. Some are stronger than others.

FACT

▷ One in five children should be wearing glasses, but they don't know it!
Ask for an eye test if:

▷ You can't see the board at school.

▷ You get lots of headaches.

▷ You can't read street signs from a car.

Some people can't get to the optician's practice for a regular check-up. This may be because they have a disability, or they are too old or ill to leave home. They can make an appointment for Riyaz to visit them at home to do an eye test.

Riyaz is about to go out on some home visits.

Everyone needs to have their eyes tested regularly, including people in prison. Once a month, Riyaz and Toni make visits to the nearby Gartree Prison. They give the inmates eye tests in the prison.

Riyaz takes a lot of eye testing equipment with him on his visits.

When a patient has an eye test, they may not know that they have a problem with their eyes, or with their health.

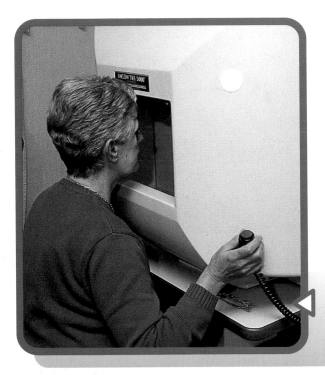

Riyaz can detect a number of medical conditions during an eye test. He uses a special "field testing" machine to find out if a patient can only see things straight in front of them. A patient with this problem may not be allowed to drive.

This "field testing" machine can show up serious illnesses in a patient, such as cancer of the brain.

Older patients might develop high pressure behind the eye. This can lead to a condition called **glaucoma**. If glaucoma is not treated, the patient could go blind.

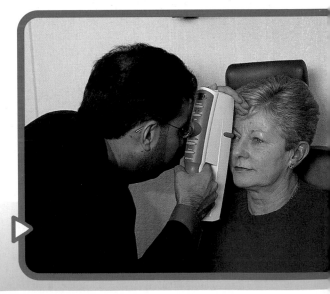

Riyaz uses a machine called a tonometer to measure eye pressure. This blows air into the patient's eye to test the pressure behind it.

When Riyaz examines an elderly patient's eyes, he looks for eye conditions such as **cataracts**. A cataract makes the lens of the eye cloudy, so it is hard for the patient to see.

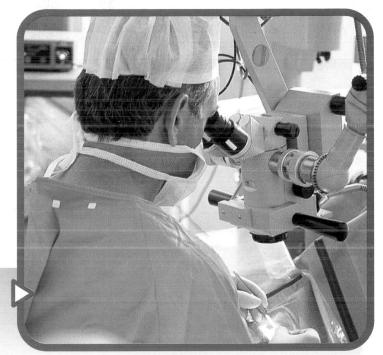

Cataracts are removed by an operation. The surgeon uses a microscope to see clearly.

Unhealthy eyes can indicate general health problems, such as high blood pressure. If Riyaz discovers something like this, he advises the patient to visit their doctor. He then writes to their doctor, to explain the situation.

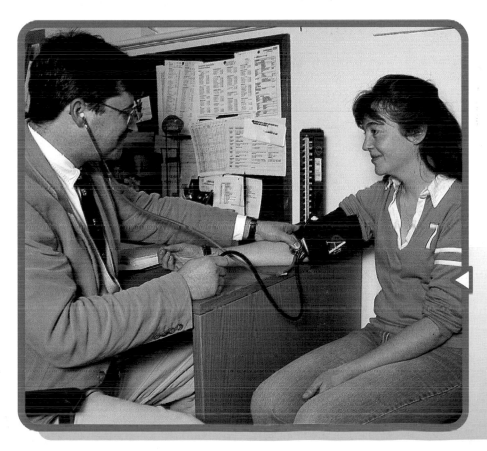

Deborah is at the doctor's, having her blood pressure checked. Riyaz told her to visit her doctor for a check-up.

⚁ It is not always easy to choose a new pair of glasses. There are so many different styles!

Toni is the dispenser. Part of her job is to help people choose new frames.
The optician's practice sells sunglasses and sports glasses as well as ordinary glasses.

Toni picks out a style that she thinks would suit Deborah.

It can be hard for people to see what they look like wearing the frames on display. This is because the frames do not have lenses in them. To solve this problem, Toni uses a digital camera.

The digital camera took photos of Deborah wearing various new frames. Deborah can now wear her old glasses to look at herself on the screen, and see what the new frames will look like on her.

Once the new glasses have been chosen, the frames have to be fitted with lenses. Toni checks the patient's lens prescription on their record card. Then she sends the frames to a laboratory to have the correct lenses fitted.

Deborah has come into the practice to pick up her new glasses.

> *Some people find it very hard to choose new frames. Sometimes they bring in their whole family to help them decide!*
> **Toni, dispenser**

Glasses are fragile and frames can break. People sometimes bring in their broken glasses to be repaired. Small problems can be fixed straightaway, but bigger repairs are sent off to be done by an expert.

Joe is doing a small repair.

■ **Contact lenses are tiny round lenses, which fit onto the surface of the eye. Some people prefer wearing them rather than glasses.**

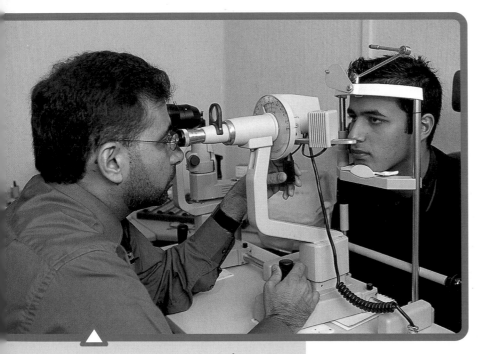

Eye tests for contact lenses are slightly different from eye tests for glasses. Contact lenses must fit perfectly onto the eye, so the patient's eye needs to be measured. To do this, Riyaz uses a machine called a keratometer.

Riyaz is measuring the shape of Karan's eye with a keratometer.

Riyaz tests the patient's eyesight in the normal way. He then puts trial contact lenses into the patient's eyes.

Riyaz puts contact lenses into Karan's eyes. The contact lenses are the right prescription for him.

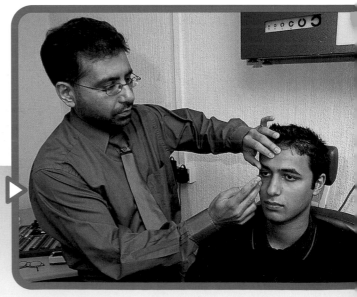

Riyaz uses a special piece of equipment to check that Karan's contact lenses fit properly. He looks into Karan's eyes with a machine called a "split-lamp microscope".

The split-lamp microscope helps Riyaz to look at the front surface of the eye.

Riyaz always checks that patients know how to look after their contact lenses. Some contact lenses have to be cleaned every day. Others are only worn for a day, and are then thrown away. These are called "daily disposable lenses".

Riyaz picks out some contact lenses for a patient. He checks the patient's records to get the right prescription.

> **People who wear contact lenses should clean them properly, and change them when they need to. Old, dirty or damaged contact lenses can cause eye infections.**
>
> **Riyaz, optometrist**

Eye hospital

🎲 **During an eye test, an optometrist may find problems that need hospital treatment.**

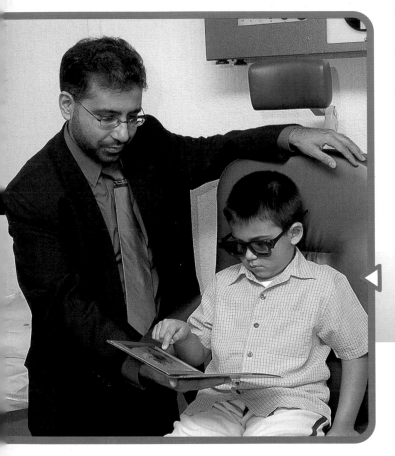

Femi has a lazy eye, and Riyaz thinks he may need an operation to correct the condition. Riyaz will write a letter to Femi's doctor, who will organise an appointment with a specialist at a hospital.

Riyaz checks to see if there has been any improvement in Femi's lazy eye since his last eye test.

Riyaz's patients are usually sent to the Leicester Royal Infirmary, which is the local hospital.

Leicester Royal Infirmary has an eye department with specially trained doctors.

Sometimes people come to the practice with eye injuries. Riyaz asks them how they hurt their eye. Then he usually gives the patient eye drops to kill any germs. Tracey had an accident in her garden and has hurt her eye.

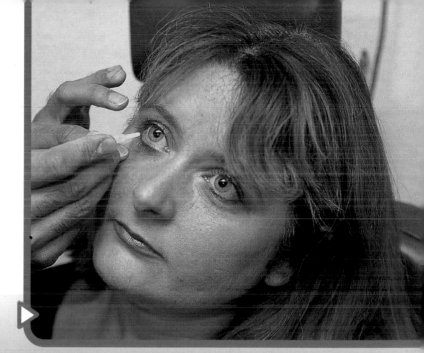

Riyaz puts some eye drops into Tracey's eyes.

If their injury is bad, Riyaz sends patients to the eye department at the Leicester Royal Infirmary. He writes a report of the incident, for the patient to give to the hospital doctors.

This is the Balmoral Building
Listed below are the Wards & Departments in this Building

	Balmoral Reception	Level 6	Wards 19, 21 & 22 Surgical Assessment Unit Vascular Studies Unit
Level 1	E N T Clinic Fracture Clinic Clinics 1 to 5 Balmoral Eye Clinic Balmoral X-ray Windsor Reception Way Out	Level 5	Wards 15, 16, 17 & 18
		Level 4	Wards 10, 11, 12 & 14 Children's Intensive Care Unit Children's Hospital School
Level 0	Physiotherapy Dept. Occupational Therapy Maxillo Facial Dept. Balmoral MRI Unit Restaurant Victoria Building	Level 3	Wards 7, 8 & 9 Kinmonth Unit Burns & Plastics
		Level 2	Adult Intensive Care Unit Day Ward Central Operating Dept.

Most of the emergencies I see are people who have had accidents when they were gardening. Often they have got a small twig caught in their eye.
Riyaz, optometrist

Patients are sent to the Balmoral Eye Clinic at the Leicester Royal Infirmary. Can you see it on this sign?

LOOKING AFTER YOUR EYES

Be careful with your eyes. They are delicate and can get damaged very easily.

1. Make regular visits to your optometrist to get your eyes checked.

2. Never look at the sun, not even through sunglasses.

3. Wear sunglasses on bright, sunny days to protect your eyes from the sun's harmful rays.

4. Don't rub your eyes if they are sore or itchy. Wash your eyes with some sterile eyewash. (If you don't have any eyewash, use water that has been boiled and then cooled.)

5. If you have an eye infection, don't spread the infection by touching your eyes. Visit your doctor as soon as possible to get medical help.

ACCIDENTS AND EMERGENCIES

If you get something small stuck in your eye, for example a speck of dust or an eyelash, ask an adult to help you get it out. It doesn't matter if you cry, because your tears will clean out your eye! Blink a lot too – that may help move the tiny speck.

A black eye is a bruise around the eye. It looks bad but it is not usually a serious injury. If you get a black eye, put a cool flannel over the bruise for about half an hour. This will help to stop the swelling.

If you cut or scratch the surface of your eye in an accident, do the following:

1. Close your eye and cover it with a clean handkerchief.

2. Do not try any first aid.

3. Phone for an ambulance, or go straight to the casualty department at the nearest hospital.

Glossary

cataract A condition where the tiny lens in the eye clouds over. If a cataract patient does not get help, they may go blind in the affected eye.

colour-blind A person who is colour-blind finds it hard to tell the difference between certain colours.

contact lenses Small, round lenses which fit directly onto the surface of the eye, to help a person see clearly.

dispenser Someone who works in an optician's practice, sorting out glasses or contact lenses.

focus When you focus on something, you adjust your eyes when looking at it so that the image is clear.

glaucoma High pressure at the back of the eye.

lazy eye The muscles in a lazy eye do not work as well as they should to make the eye focus on an object.

lens (lenses) The lens of an eye focuses light as it comes in through the pupil so that it falls onto the retina (see picture on p.9).

Lenses in glasses are curved pieces of glass or plastic that work with the lens in the eye to help people focus on things.

long-sighted Someone who is long-sighted can't see things that are nearby very clearly. This is because light focuses behind the retina at the back of the eye.

optical equipment The tools and instruments an optometrist uses to test people's eyesight.

optician's practice The place where you go for an eye test and to buy glasses and contact lenses.

optometrist Someone who is qualified to test eyesight, fit contact lenses and sell glasses.

patient record The information an optometrist needs to know about a patient's eyesight.

prescription A description of the type and strength of lenses a patient needs.

pupil The pupil is the small black hole in the centre of the eye.

retina The area at the back of the eye where light is focused.

short-sighted Someone who is short-sighted is unable to see things in the distance very clearly. This is because light focuses in front of the retina at the back of the eye.

squint A person with a squint can't make both eyes look together in the same direction.

Further information

To find out more about how to look after your eyes, you could visit this website:

www.allaboutvision.com/parents

The Eyecare Trust provides information about eyesight and how to look after your eyes.

Visit the Eyecare Trust website at: www.eye-care.org.uk

To find out more about how the eye works and caring for your eyesight in Australia, visit:

www.zamazam.com.au/eyes

Note to parents and teachers: Every effort has been made by the Publishers to ensure that these websites are suitable for children; that they are of the highest educational value, and that they contain no inappropriate or offensive material. However, because of the nature of the Internet, it is impossible to guarantee that the contents of these sites will not be altered. We strongly advise that Internet access is supervised by a responsible adult.

Index